Original title:
Embracing Myself

Copyright © 2024 Swan Charm
All rights reserved.

Author: Linda Leevike
ISBN HARDBACK: 978-9916-89-961-8
ISBN PAPERBACK: 978-9916-89-962-5
ISBN EBOOK: 978-9916-89-963-2

The Gospel of Inner Harmony

In the quiet heart, peace does dwell,
Whispers of love, a sacred spell.
Harmony sings where turmoil flowed,
In the stillness, true grace bestowed.

To seek within, the light we find,
A gentle voice, our path aligned.
In humble prayer, our souls unite,
Illuminated by divine light.

Forgiveness blooms in tender care,
Casting aside the heavy snare.
Each step in faith, a soothing balm,
In unity, the spirit's calm.

With open hearts, we gather near,
In every moment, love draws near.
A tapestry of sacred art,
We weave together, heart by heart.

Let gratitude rise like morning dew,
In each exchange, a promise new.
In joy and sorrow, find the chord,
Inner harmony, our true reward.

Reverence for the Inner Light

In silence deep, the spirit glows,
A spark of grace that gently flows.
With every breath, the truth we seek,
The whispering heart, so soft, so meek.

In prayerful gaze, the soul ascends,
A guiding light that never ends.
Through trials faced and storms we braved,
The inner calm is always saved.

Illuminating the Shadows

In darkest nights, the light breaks through,
Each shadow cast, a lesson true.
The flicker guides the weary soul,
Restoring hope, it makes us whole.

With every tear, a light is born,
From scars and wounds, our spirits worn.
Thus in the gloom, we find our grace,
Illuminated, we meet His face.

The Pilgrimage Within

Each step I take, my heart aligned,
A sacred journey, purpose defined.
With open arms, I seek the divine,
In every moment, love will shine.

Mountains high and valleys low,
Through faith and trust, I learn to grow.
With every turn, horizons wide,
I find the peace that lives inside.

The Mosaic of My Faith

In vibrant hues, the pieces join,
A tapestry of soul's own coin.
Each fragment tells a story clear,
Of hope and love, dispelling fear.

With humble heart, I weave my thread,
A prayer for all, for those long dead.
In every shade, a glimpse of grace,
The sacred dance, my warm embrace.

Worship in Quietude

In hush of dawn, we gather near,
With whispers soft, our hearts sincere.
In quietude, our spirits rise,
To touch the veil that splits the skies.

Each breath a prayer, each thought a light,
In stillness found, our souls take flight.
With humble hearts, we seek the grace,
Of love divine in sacred space.

The Sanctuary of Silence

In silence deep, the spirit thrives,
Where thoughts dissolve and peace arrives.
Within this sacred, hallowed ground,
The whispered truths of God abound.

The echoes of a holy song,
In every soul where we belong.
We pause to hear the heart's pure call,
In the sanctuary, we stand tall.

The Divine Legacy of Me

In every tear, a story flows,
Of grace bestowed, as spirit grows.
Embracing light, the shadows flee,
A tapestry that reflects me.

With every step, my faith I weave,
In sacred trust, I dare believe.
The legacy of love I share,
A testament to the One who cares.

Prayers from the Depths of My Being

With every heartbeat, prayers arise,
From depths untold, beneath the skies.
In quiet caverns of my soul,
The longing seeks to make me whole.

In fervent whispers, I lay bare,
The hopes and dreams, my every prayer.
From depths unknown, I cry and yearn,
For love divine, my heart's return.

The Sacred Mirror

In the silence, truth convenes,
Reflections dance in holy Light.
In every gaze, divinity gleams,
The soul's whisper, pure and bright.

Face the depths, confront the grace,
In shadows, find the sacred call.
Each flaw embraced, a sacred trace,
The spirit rises, free from thrall.

In every tear, a lesson glows,
Forgive the past, unwrap the pain.
Transcend the fears that once arose,
Rebirth from loss, share in the gain.

The mirror holds a timeless view,
A canvas vast of love divine.
In every heart, a chance to renew,
Where all souls flourish, intertwine.

A Journey Within the Temple

Inside the stillness, whispers rise,
A journey starts within the heart.
Each step leads to the skies,
In this sacred space, souls part.

The walls echo with sacred lore,
Stories woven in the air.
With each heartbeat, spirits soar,
Divine embrace, beyond compare.

Seek the altar where fears dissolve,
In silence, listen, feel the way.
A mystery wrapped to solve,
In humble light, the shadows sway.

Within the temple, grace ignites,
Each soul reflects the heavenly flame.
In unity, we see the sights,
A journey of love, never the same.

The Altar of Self-Acceptance

Upon the altar, love unfolds,
A gentle truth, acceptance found.
In flaws and strengths, the heart beholds,
Each piece a treasure, unbound.

Lay down your burdens, free your mind,
Trust in the path that you create.
In every heartbeat, wisdom finds,
A sacred bond that won't abate.

Embrace the scars, the battles fought,
With every challenge, brighter you shine.
In every lesson, love is sought,
A journey sweet, a grand design.

Stand tall before the mirror's grace,
A sacred ritual, pure and right.
In loving self, we find our place,
The altar shines, a guiding light.

Reverent Whispers of the Soul

In quiet moments, whispers sing,
Voices echo from the deep.
The spirit's song takes wing,
In sacred secrets, still we weep.

Each revelation, gentle breeze,
Carrying prayers through the air.
As the heart bends with ease,
Beneath the weight, love's tender care.

In the stillness, truth unfolds,
Reverent whispers soft and clear.
The fabric of life, a tapestry bold,
In every thread, the sacred near.

Listen closely, to the soul's refrain,
A melody of grace divine.
In unity, joy and pain,
Intertwined, the stars align.

Blessings from the Heart's Altar

In stillness, whispers of grace,
A soft touch upon the soul's space.
With every prayer, hope takes flight,
Illuminating borders of night.

In gratitude, we lift our hands,
United in love, our heart understands.
Each blessing high, like birds in the sky,
Returning to us, like the sun's warm sigh.

Through trials faced, we find our way,
Guided by faith through the fray.
With every heartbeat, sacred and true,
A melody of life, fresh as the dew.

So let us gather, all spirits aligned,
In the warmth of acceptance, kindness defined.
Eternal gratitude, a sacred art,
In the blessings bestowed from the heart's altar.

The Divine Call of Self-Realization

In the mirror of truth, we stand,
Reflecting the love of a guiding hand.
Awakened souls, striving to be,
The essence of what we are meant to see.

Through trials and errors, wisdom unfolds,
A journey of beauty, relentless and bold.
In silence we hear the inner voice,
A divine whisper urging our choice.

As shadows fade, and light finds its way,
We embrace the dawn of a brand new day.
Self-realization, a path pure and bright,
Illuminating hearts in the stillness of night.

With love as our guide, let us walk tall,
Embracing the truth in the divine call.
A symphony of spirits, united and free,
In each sacred step, we find our decree.

Prayers of the Unsung Self

In the quiet corners of weary hearts,
Lies a rhythm known, where silence starts.
Prayers whispered low, seldom heard,
Echoing softly, each heartfelt word.

For the unsung self, we seek to ignite,
A flame of compassion, burning bright.
In hidden places, dreams begin to bloom,
Transcending the darkness, dispelling the gloom.

With every inhale, we summon our might,
In the dance of existence, we choose to fight.
From depths uncharted, our voices will rise,
For the unsung self, we reach for the skies.

In unity's embrace, our souls become whole,
A symphony of spirits plays deep in our soul.
Let the prayers take flight, like doves set free,
The unsung self flourishing, eternally.

The Sacred Dance of Acceptance

In the circle of life, we twirl and sway,
Embracing the moments, come what may.
With open arms, we greet each fate,
In the sacred dance, love will await.

For acceptance leads us to peace profound,
In every heartbeat, a new truth found.
We release our burdens, let spirits soar,
In the rhythm of grace, forever more.

With every step, the path unfolds,
In the laughter of joy, and the wisdom of old.
Dancing to a song, pure and divine,
In acceptance, we flourish, eternally entwined.

As the world spins on, let us hold tight,
To the sacred dance igniting our light.
With each breath taken, we rise above,
In the dance of acceptance, we find our love.

Beneath the Cloak of Illusions

In shadows deep, truth lies concealed,
The heart must seek what is revealed.
With faith as light, we pierce the veil,
In quiet whispers, love will prevail.

The world's facade, a fleeting show,
Yet in our hearts, the blessings flow.
Each prayer we speak, a seed of grace,
To lift the soul, find our true place.

Beneath the cloak, in silence dwell,
The sacred pulse, the ancient tell.
Awake the spirit, from its slumber,
With every beat, hear heaven's thunder.

Trust in the path, though dark it seems,
For light will guide, fulfill our dreams.
Beneath the surface, a river streams,
Carrying hopes on angel's beams.

The Sacred Texts of My Life

Within these pages, whispers trace,
The journey marked by love and grace.
Each chapter written, a tale unfolds,
In sacred texts, my spirit holds.

Lessons learned in sacred flow,
In every joy, in every woe.
The ink of faith bleeds strong and true,
Guiding me onward, forever new.

In quiet moments, wisdom speaks,
In humble hearts, the truth we seek.
With every word, a prayer takes flight,
Illuminating the darkest night.

Turning the leaves, I find my way,
In sacred scripts, I choose to stay.
Each line a beacon, bright and bold,
In life's embrace, my story told.

The sacred texts, a map divine,
In every heart, a thread we twine.
Together woven, a tapestry,
Our lives reflect eternity.

Footprints on the Path to Wholeness

With every step on hallowed ground,
In quiet echoes, love is found.
Footprints lead where spirits soar,
Awakening hearts to evermore.

Each mark, a story, a lesson learned,
In trials faced, the soul's heart burned.
Along this path, we yearn and strive,
To find the light, keep faith alive.

In unity, we walk this way,
Guided by grace, come what may.
Hand in hand with the divine,
We search for wholeness, pure and sublime.

As seasons change and pathways bend,
Each footprint left, a sacred blend.
The journey's gift, in every glance,
Awakens love, ignites the dance.

Meditations on the Self's Sanctuary

In stillness found, the spirit breathes,
A sacred space, where truth bequeaths.
In quiet refuge, wisdom glows,
The self's sanctuary, where love flows.

Each thought a prayer, each breath a song,
In this stillness, we belong.
As shadows fade, the light draws near,
In every heartbeat, divine is clear.

In contemplation, we rest our hearts,
Within the silence, the journey starts.
Embracing shadows, we find the light,
In unity's grace, we rise in flight.

The sanctuary whispers peace so true,
In every moment, life anew.
With every glance, we see the whole,
In love's embrace, we heal the soul.

The Altar of Authenticity

In stillness, I find my truth,
A light that guides my way.
With every breath, I embrace,
The path where I shall stay.

At the altar of my soul,
I lay my fears to rest.
Each moment, a sacred vow,
To honor my own quest.

Vows whispered to the night,
With stars as my witness.
I rise from shadows long,
Embracing my own richness.

The whispers of the heart,
Echo in the silence loud.
I stand, steadfast in grace,
Amongst the gathered crowd.

With every tear that falls,
A seed of courage grows.
I walk the road of self,
Where authenticity flows.

A Covenant with My Soul

In sacred trust, I bind,
My spirit to this vow.
I promise to be kind,
To honor self right now.

Through sun and shadow's dance,
I seek the light within.
With every fleeting chance,
A new beginning begins.

Beneath the weight of doubt,
I rise, I find my wings.
With hope that sings about,
The love that always clings.

In moments of despair,
I whisper to the skies.
My soul, a gentle prayer,
In truth, my spirit flies.

Bound in this strong embrace,
I venture through the night.
With faith, I run my race,
And move towards the light.

Divine Reflections

In mirrors of the heart,
I see the spark of grace.
Each flaw, a work of art,
Each tear, a tender trace.

Reflections of the soul,
In shadows that may fall.
With every whisper, whole,
I hear the sacred call.

Illuminated threads,
We weave through joy and pain.
Life's tapestry widespread,
In beauty, none is vain.

Walk softly on this ground,
Where love's pure light is found.
In echoes, truth resounds,
In silence, hearts abound.

Within the depths of night,
Stars twinkle with a sigh.
Divine reflections bright,
As dreams ascend the sky.

The Prayer of Self-Love

In the quiet of my heart,
I whisper words divine.
A prayer that sets apart,
The love that's truly mine.

With every breath I take,
I honor who I am.
No longer shall I break,
From love's celestial plan.

Embracing all my scars,
A testament of grace.
Each flaw, a shining star,
Reflecting in this space.

Through trials, I shall rise,
With courage and with fire.
In faith, I touch the skies,
And bless my heart's desire.

This prayer, my sacred call,
To love both near and far.
In unity, we fall,
And shine like every star.

A Sacred Journey Inward

In quiet whispers, hearts begin,
A path of light where love flows thin.
In sacred silence, souls ignite,
The journey inward, pure and bright.

With every step, we shed our fears,
Embracing grace throughout the years.
In the depths, the spirit dances,
In the stillness, hope enhances.

The mirror reflects, a truth so clear,
In shadows deep, we find our cheer.
In the embrace of kindness, we learn,
A sacred flame, we take our turn.

Through valleys low and mountains high,
With faith as wings, we learn to fly.
In prayerful thoughts, we gain our aim,
To honor truth in God's own name.

As we ascend, we leave behind,
The weight of doubt, the chains that bind.
In oneness, we walk hand in hand,
In sacred light, we firmly stand.

The Holy Tapestry of Existence

Threads of compassion, intertwined,
A fabric rich, where love's defined.
In every color, dreams reside,
The holy tapestry, souls abide.

With gentle hands, we weave the grace,
In every corner, God's embrace.
Each stitch a story, woven tight,
In this design, we find the light.

Through laughter shared and tears we shed,
The sacred loom, where all are led.
In harmony, we find our peace,
From love's own cradle, joys increase.

The universe sings, in choir it speaks,
In sacred moments, truth uniquely peaks.
As stars align, our paths converge,
From life's great frame, we will emerge.

In gratitude, we spin our fate,
A tapestry of love, so great.
With every thread, we stand as one,
In holy unity, our journey's begun.

The Battlefield of Belonging

In the vale where shadows creep,
Hearts cry out, their secrets keep.
In every struggle, strength we find,
A battlefield of heart and mind.

We gather courage, side by side,
In the depths, our fears abide.
With faith as armor, we face the fight,
For in our souls, there shines a light.

The voices clash, but truth remains,
Through storms of doubt, we break our chains.
A sacred bond in every scar,
Through trials faced, we heal the war.

In unity, our spirits soar,
With every battle, we seek more.
Across divides, we seek to understand,
In love's own grace, we take our stand.

Together, we rise, hand in hand,
In this great struggle, we will withstand.
For belonging's gift is love's embrace,
On this battlefield, we find our place.

Glories of Self-Discovery

In the stillness, truth unfolds,
In whispered dreams, our spirit molds.
With open hearts, we seek the way,
In glories bright, we find our play.

Each moment treasured, lessons learned,
In every sorrow, passion burned.
The quest for self, a sacred art,
Awakens wonders, deep in heart.

With every scar, a story told,
In battles fought, our spirits bold.
We rise with wisdom, grace bestowed,
In glories found, our journey flowed.

Embracing flaws, we start anew,
In love's reflection, we see it true.
The dance of life, our souls engage,
In self-discovery, we find our sage.

As stardust flows through time and space,
In unity, we find our place.
The joys of knowing, hearts revealed,
In wondrous glories, we are healed.

Seraphic Whispers

In the stillness, angels sing,
Their voices soft, a holy ring.
Eternal truths in whispered grace,
In every heart, they find their place.

Heaven's light, a warm embrace,
Guiding souls through time and space.
In quiet prayer, we find the way,
To live in love, day by day.

The gentle breeze, a calming breath,
Awakens life within, not death.
In gratitude, our spirits soar,
United, we seek and adore.

Hope arises, like the dawn,
A sacred song, we carry on.
In seraphic whispers, we unite,
Together embraced in purest light.

A Celestial Dance of Discovery

Stars above in cosmic dance,
Inviting us to take a chance.
Twilight dreams and visions bright,
Lead us onward, hearts alight.

With every step, a story told,
Of love and courage, brave and bold.
In unity, we find our song,
Together, we truly belong.

The universe, a sacred pen,
Writing love for all, again.
In every heartbeat, life resides,
Celestial whispers, ancient guides.

As sun and moon embrace the sky,
We raise our voices, never shy.
In this dance, our spirits bloom,
In harmony, we break the gloom.

The Fruit of Inner Peace

In silence deep, the soul takes flight,
Harvesting joy from inner light.
With whispered prayers on gentle winds,
The path of peace, our spirit mends.

Calm waters flow, reflecting grace,
In every heart, a sacred space.
With every breath, we seek and find,
The fruit of peace within our mind.

Amidst the chaos, find the still,
In trust and faith, we bend our will.
With love, we nurture seeds so small,
And watch them blossom, one and all.

In unity, we cultivate
A harvest rich, a life of fate.
The fruit of peace, a sacred bond,
Together, we grow and respond.

My Spirit, a Sacred Scroll

My spirit whispers, deep and true,
A sacred scroll for me and you.
In every joy and hidden pain,
The lessons learned, the love we gain.

With every line, a story penned,
Of grace and mercy that won't end.
In faith, we turn each fragile page,
Embracing hope, we are the sage.

A tapestry of woven dreams,
In unity, our spirit gleams.
In quietude, the heart can hear,
The sacred truths that banish fear.

Through trials faced and battles fought,
In every moment, wisdom's sought.
My spirit's scroll, a map divine,
Leading all to love's design.

Heavenly Harmonies

In whispers soft, the angels sing,
Of joy divine, and hope they bring.
Through clouds of grace, their voices soar,
In sacred realms, forevermore.

With every note, a soul is blessed,
In harmony, we find our rest.
A symphony of love unfolds,
The Secrets of the heart retold.

In prayerful silence, hearts unite,
With faith we walk, through day and night.
The heavenly choir guides our way,
In trust, we find the light of day.

Each sacred breath, a holy vow,
In every moment, here and now.
A dance of spirits, intertwined,
In life's embrace, the truth we find.

Let praises rise, like incense sweet,
In gratitude, our hearts shall meet.
For in this bond, we touch the sky,
As love transcends, we learn to fly.

Ode to My Own Temple

In silence deep, my spirit speaks,
With every prayer, my heart it seeks.
The walls of love, a sacred space,
Reflecting light, my soul's embrace.

Within my chest, a holy flame,
A whispered truth, I know my name.
With every breath, I build the hall,
My inner peace, my truest call.

In moments still, I find the key,
To set my spirit free, to be.
In worship's glow, I stand alone,
Yet in my heart, I find the throne.

Unfurling dreams, like petals bloom,
Inside my temple, love consumes.
Each heartbeat echoes sacred rhyme,
A timeless dance, to grace and mime.

In solitude, I form my prayer,
In whispers soft, the world I care.
With open hands, I greet the dawn,
As faith abounds, I journey on.

The Light of Understanding

In shadows deep, the truth awaits,
A guiding star, that love creates.
Through trials faced, the heart compels,
With every doubt, the spirit dwells.

In moments frail, the light breaks through,
Illuminating paths anew.
With eyes wide open, we can see,
The boundless grace, that sets us free.

In every sorrow, wisdom grows,
Revealing what the spirit knows.
Compassion's touch, a sacred gift,
In understanding, we shall lift.

In unity, our voices blend,
A chorus strong, the will to mend.
Through love we rise, beyond the night,
In every heart, the spark of light.

With gentle steps, we walk the way,
Embracing hope, come what may.
For in the soul, the light resides,
In every heart, true love abides.

The Sacrificial Journey to Self

To seek the truth, I must let go,
Of fears and doubts, the seeds they sew.
In humble quests, I search within,
To find the source, where love begins.

With heavy heart, I lay my pain,
In surrender, the spirit gains.
Each tear I shed, a step I take,
Towards the dawn, for freedom's sake.

In every trial, the lesson calls,
To rise anew, as darkness falls.
With faith as guide, I face the storm,
In every loss, the spirit's form.

In quiet depths, I learn to trust,
The sacred fire, beneath the dust.
Through sacrifice, my essence glows,
In letting go, the wisdom flows.

Embracing grace, I find the way,
To give my heart, and thus to pray.
In every breath, my soul, it strives,
For in this journey, love survives.

In Praise of My Existence

I awake each dawn with grace,
Life's whispers dance upon my face.
A sacred breath within my chest,
In this existence, I am blessed.

Each step I take, a prayer's song,
In a world where I belong.
With every heartbeat, love unfolds,
A tapestry of stories told.

In trials faced, His light I find,
Guiding me through paths unkind.
In joys and sorrows, He remains,
In life's embrace, my spirit gains.

I celebrate this precious gift,
In quiet moments, my soul lifts.
Each blessing born from pains endured,
In praise of self, my heart is cured.

Through mountains high and valleys low,
In every breath, His presence flows.
With gratitude, I sing my song,
For in my existence, I am strong.

The Holy Land of Acceptance

In silent grace, I find my peace,
Where judgments fade and worries cease.
A sacred space where hearts align,
In acceptance, my soul will shine.

Each moment shared, a gentle prayer,
In unity, we breathe the air.
No walls between us, only love,
A holy land, blessed from above.

With open arms, we welcome all,
In kindness spoken, we stand tall.
Together woven, hearts entwined,
In this embrace, true strength we find.

Through trials faced, we learn and grow,
In acceptance, our spirits flow.
A journey shared, hand in hand,
In the holy land where we all stand.

Let go of fears, release the pain,
In this space, we all remain.
For in acceptance, we shall see,
The beauty of our unity.

A Divine Embrace of Wholeness

In the stillness of the night,
I find His love, so pure and bright.
Wrapped in grace, my heart is whole,
A divine embrace, my sacred soul.

Each flaw I carry, seen as light,
In shadows dark, I find my sight.
For every piece of me, divine,
In wholeness, I begin to shine.

In every struggle, strength I find,
A symphony of heart and mind.
With faithful hands, He molds my clay,
In His embrace, I find my way.

Together as one, we rise above,
In the arms of everlasting love.
No fear remains, just truth unveiled,
In wholeness found, my spirit hailed.

Each day a gift, a chance to be,
In this embrace, I come to see.
That I am whole, beloved, free,
A divine reflection, eternally.

The Unfolding Scroll of My Story

Each chapter written, a tale to share,
With ink of love, and endless care.
In trials faced, my courage grows,
The unfolding scroll of life bestows.

From gentle whispers to roaring tides,
In every moment, a truth abides.
With every turn, a lesson learned,
In sacred pages, my spirit yearns.

In laughter shared and tears embraced,
The tapestry of life is traced.
A story woven with threads of light,
In every struggle, beauty ignites.

Let patience guide me through the strife,
For every ending births new life.
In the scroll of time, my spirit flies,
With faith as wings, I reach the skies.

Each verse I write, a prayerful breath,
In love and hope, beyond mere death.
The story's chapters will always ring,
In the heart of all, new life we bring.

Celestial Sojourns

In quiet grace, the stars do shine,
Guiding souls on paths divine.
With whispers soft, the heavens sing,
Of love and hope, eternal spring.

Through trials faced in darkened night,
Faith's gentle glow brings forth the light.
Each step we take, in sacred trust,
Unites our hearts, as one we must.

The moon's embrace, a tender kiss,
In nature's arms, we find our bliss.
Each journey shared, a blessed song,
In unity, we all belong.

With every breath, the spirit soars,
Beyond the veil to open doors.
Celestial realms, we touch and feel,
In love's embrace, our wounds will heal.

Together lifted, hand in hand,
We journey forth, a holy band.
In every star, a spark of grace,
Eternal light, our guiding place.

The Beatitudes of Self-Revelation

Blessed are those who seek to know,
In humble hearts, the truth will grow.
The meek shall rise, the lost shall find,
A loving peace, forever kind.

With open eyes, we glimpse the dawn,
The beauty found in every fawn.
Through trials faced, our spirits shine,
In quiet whispers, the divine.

Blessed are those who mourn with grace,
For joy is found in love's embrace.
The gentle soul, the pure of heart,
Shall witness beauty set apart.

With hearts aflame, we walk the way,
In every night, we seek the day.
To share our gifts, to lift the weak,
In love's own language, we shall speak.

Seek not the riches of this world,
But treasures found in love unfurled.
In every kindness, grace bestowed,
The path of light is surely showed.

Faith in the Face of Doubt

When shadows loom and hopes seem bare,
We lift our eyes, the weight we bear.
In quiet prayer, our hearts confide,
For truth shall bloom, where fears reside.

Through tempest fierce, our spirits rise,
In darkest hour, we seek the skies.
Each doubt we face, a stepping stone,
To strength renewed, we are not alone.

With every breath, we claim our ground,
In faith unyielding, love is found.
The heart's resolve in trials pressed,
Will guide us forth, we are blessed.

Embrace the doubt, let it ignite,
A flame of hope, a beacon bright.
In all we lose, remember this:
With faith alive, we dwell in bliss.

So hold the light, let shadows flee,
In every heart, the truth shall be.
With courage bold, we face the day,
Faith in our hearts, we find our way.

The Journey Home

In every step, our souls embark,
A quest for love, igniting spark.
With open hearts, we wander free,
Toward endless grace, our destiny.

Through valleys deep and mountains high,
We lift our voices to the sky.
In every joy, in every tear,
The journey home draws ever near.

With gentle hands, we heal the past,
In every moment, love holds fast.
Together bound by grace we roam,
In every heart, we find our home.

The path of peace, a sacred thread,
Through darkest nights, where dreams are bred.
With spirits joined in sacred hymn,
We walk in light, our hearts not dim.

So fear not, dear ones, the road ahead,
In every step, our love is spread.
For in each soul, a flame shall burn,
To guide us back, to home, return.

Hymns of Vulnerability and Strength

In shadows cast, we find our light,
Each tear a spark, a sacred sight.
With open hearts, we stand so brave,
Embracing love, the soul to save.

In whispered prayers, our voices rise,
With humble spirits, we touch the skies.
Each flaw laid bare, a mark of grace,
Together bound, we find our place.

When storms arise, and fears take flight,
We seek the dawn, the path of right.
In every fall, a chance to grow,
Through every wound, the love will show.

As hands are joined in faith so pure,
We heal the world with hearts secure.
In unity, our trust enchained,
Through sacred bonds, our strength regained.

In silence deep, our whispers blend,
A chorus true, where spirits mend.
With faith our guide, and love entwined,
We walk this road, with hope designed.

Prayers of Authenticity

Lord, help us show our truest face,
In every flaw, find a sweet grace.
With every doubt, ignite the light,
In honest hearts, our souls take flight.

Guide us to speak with voices clear,
To share our truths, dismiss our fear.
In sacred trust, let spirits blend,
For every path, Your love will mend.

In moments small, where doubt may grow,
Let courage rise, let kindness flow.
With open hearts, we face the day,
In every breath, Your truth we say.

With footsteps firm, we seek the way,
To live each moment, come what may.
Embracing life, both pain and cheer,
In each heartbeat, Your presence near.

Together, Lord, we lift our prayer,
In vulnerability, we bare.
With souls unmasked, our spirits soar,
In every truth, we're evermore.

The Pilgrimage to Inner Peace

With every step, we seek the calm,
In nature's arms, a soothing balm.
Through winding paths and valleys deep,
We journey forth, our spirits leap.

The sunlight shines on weary feet,
In quiet spaces, pulse and beat.
We listen close to whispers kind,
With each soft breath, our hearts unwind.

In solitude, the truth is found,
Within the stillness, love resounds.
Each moment cherished, none in vain,
With grace we rise, through joy and pain.

As rivers flow, so too do we,
Embracing change, the mystery.
In unity, our hearts collide,
We walk this path, with faith as guide.

In every dawn, a chance to see,
The beauty of simplicity.
Our pilgrimage, a sacred art,
Finding peace deep in the heart.

Echoes of the Sacred Breath

Within the silence, whispers call,
The sacred breath, embracing all.
In every sigh, the spirit flows,
In unity, our essence knows.

As mountains rise and rivers bend,
We find the strength that does not end.
With every heartbeat, truth resounds,
In gentle waves, our love abounds.

In moments worn, where souls connect,
We gather hope, we love, reflect.
In shared communion, grace ignites,
In every prayer, the heart ignites.

Breath of the earth, and sky so wide,
In sacred space, we turn the tide.
With open arms, we embrace change,
In each new dawn, we rearrange.

As echoes fade, new sounds arise,
In harmony, the spirit flies.
In every breath, a promise made,
With faith and love, we'll never fade.

A Pilgrim's Heart: Journey to Acceptance

In the silence of night, I tread my way,
Seeking solace beneath the stars' sway.
Each step a whisper, each pause a prayer,
In the heart of the journey, I find my care.

With every stumble, a lesson unfolds,
In the warmth of the light, my spirit holds.
Through valleys of doubt, and mountains of grace,
I embrace my path, each challenge I face.

Mountains may rise, as the storms roll in,
Yet the peace within grows, a treasure within.
In acceptance I bloom, like flowers in spring,
A pilgrim's heart learns to softly sing.

So I walk on this road, with faith as my guide,
Each step a testament, a holy stride.
With a heart full of love, and hands open wide,
In the journey of acceptance, I forever abide.

The Holy Bond with My Spirit

In the stillness of dawn, my soul does arise,
Connected to the heavens, a bond that never dies.
In prayer, I find strength, in silence, I see,
The holy connection, just my spirit and me.

Through trials and storms, my spirit remains,
A guiding presence, through joys and pains.
With every heartbeat, a rhythm divine,
In this holy bond, my essence does shine.

The whispers of angels, I feel in the air,
A sacred reminder, that always is there.
In the depths of my being, a light ever bright,
In union we dance, with the stars in the night.

With faith as my vessel, I sail the vast sea,
Together with my spirit, I am truly free.
In each breath I take, the divine I embrace,
In the holy bond, I find my true place.

Chants of the Inner Sanctuary

Within the stillness, my spirit does sing,
Chants of the inner, where joy takes wing.
In the depths of silence, a melody grows,
Echoing softly, where true peace flows.

In the sacred chamber of my quiet heart,
I gather the fragments, no longer apart.
Each note a reminder of love shining bright,
Chants of the inner, a beacon of light.

Through moments of darkness, I find my refrain,
A symphony woven with love's gentle chain.
In the echoes of calm, I discover my worth,
Chants of the inner, a song of rebirth.

In unity found, I rise and I stand,
With each sacred chant, I embrace the divine hand.
In the sanctuary's heart, forever I'll dwell,
Chants of the inner, a love I can tell.

The Celestial Symphony of Self

In the vast expanse of the evening's grace,
I listen to whispers from a faraway place.
The symphony calls in a celestial tone,
Each note a reminder that I am not alone.

With stars as my witnesses, I rise and I sing,
In harmony woven, my spirit takes wing.
The music around me, a dance of the soul,
In this celestial play, I feel wholly whole.

As the moonlight shines down, embracing my heart,
I join in the chorus, each voice plays a part.
The symphony swells, in a vibrant array,
In the celestial rhythm, I find my own way.

With gratitude flowing like rivers of light,
The celestial notes guide me through the night.
In the sacred cadence of existence, I dwell,
In the symphony of self, I find all is well.

Beneath the Shroud of Doubt

In shadows deep where faith may wane,
I seek Thy light, amidst the pain.
With whispers soft, Thy grace does call,
To lift my heart, to rise, not fall.

Each question swirls like autumn leaves,
Yet in the stillness, my spirit cleaves.
Thy promises, a guiding star,
Remind me, Lord, just who You are.

When storms arise and hope feels lost,
I clutch Thy love, regardless of cost.
Beneath the shroud, hope starts to shine,
In every doubt, I find the divine.

Help me to stand, through trials faced,
In every tear, Thy love embraced.
The path unknown, a sacred trust,
In Thee, O Lord, I place my lust.

So let the doubts come as they may,
I'll walk with Thee, come what may.
For in Thy arms, I truly live,
To You, my heart, I freely give.

The Pilgrimage to Wholeness

In every step, a sacred quest,
To find the peace, my soul's true rest.
With every breath, I journey on,
Towards the light, 'neath rising dawn.

The road is steep, the path unsure,
Yet, Lord, I know, You are my cure.
Each moment shared upon this trek,
Brings me closer, no need to fret.

Through valleys low and mountains high,
I lift my hands, I raise my cry.
To seek the wholeness, pure and bright,
In every shadow, find Your light.

The trials faced, they shape the soul,
With Thee, O Lord, I am made whole.
In unity with all that's true,
My heart, my life, belong to You.

As pilgrims tread on sacred ground,
In silence, let Thy grace abound.
For in the journey, joy unfolds,
As every heart seeks to be told.

Anointing My Spirit

With oils of grace, my spirit seeks,
A touch divine, in silence speaks.
In every droplet, healing flows,
In every breath, Your mercy glows.

The hands of love, they come to bless,
Each weary heart, You soothe and press.
Anointing me with sacred care,
In humble prayer, my burdens share.

O Lord, anoint my lips to sing,
Of all the hope that You can bring.
In every note, Your truth I find,
A melody that stirs the blind.

In whispered prayers that rise like smoke,
In every word, Your promise spoke.
So wash me clean, O Lord, anew,
Anoint my spirit, true and blue.

With every tear, Your love impart,
In all my shadows, light impart.
Through trials faced, I gleam and shine,
In spirit, Lord, forever Thine.

The Holy Embrace of Being

In stillness deep, I find my peace,
In holy breath, all worries cease.
Your presence, Lord, a warm embrace,
In every moment, see Your face.

As petals fold from morning dew,
I bloom within, with love anew.
In every heartbeat, whispered song,
You cradle me, where I belong.

With arms outstretched, I feel You near,
In quiet dawn, I shed my fear.
Each simple breath, a prayer unfolds,
In sacred hush, Your love enfolds.

The soul that dances in Your light,
Finds joy and peace, dispels the night.
In every tear, a truth shall gleam,
Through love's embrace, I live the dream.

So let me bask in this embrace,
A holy touch, a sacred space.
In every moment, make me whole,
In You, I find my truest soul.

Light Illuminates the Path

In shadows deep, the light does shine,
Guiding souls through trails divine.
With every step, a hand is near,
Whispering hopes to calm our fear.

The dawn breaks forth, a radiant beam,
Bringing forth the sweetest dream.
Each moment glows, the heart takes flight,
Embracing love, dispelling night.

In faith we walk, through trials vast,
Knowing well, the shadows pass.
With open hearts, we seek His grace,
Finding strength in every place.

Through valleys low, our spirits rise,
Trusting in the wise and wise.
For light will lead, and hope will stay,
Illuminating every way.

At journey's end, His arms await,
Embracing those who seek His fate.
In light we find the path so true,
For every step brings us to You.

From Ashes to Grace

In the quiet night, a fire burns,
From ash and smoke, the spirit yearns.
Grace emerges from broken schemes,
In shattered dreams, we find new themes.

Like phoenix rising, hope takes flight,
From depths of sorrow, into the light.
Every scar holds a sacred tale,
Of love reborn when we prevail.

With open hands, we gather shards,
Transforming pain in life's regards.
Each tear we shed, a chance to grow,
In fields of faith, our hearts bestow.

In gentle whispers, we are taught,
That every loss is never naught.
From ashes, beauty finds its place,
And in our hearts, we find His grace.

For in each moment, strength is found,
As love uplifts from hallowed ground.
From ashes, rise, and learn to trust,
In faith and grace, we are robust.

The Blessing of Vulnerability

In openness, our hearts unite,
Casting away the shrouds of night.
For in our flaws, true beauty glows,
A garden blooms where love bestows.

Each whispered prayer, a tender plea,
In sacred truth, we learn to see.
A gentle soul, unmasked and bare,
Reveals the strength in every care.

With every crack, the light breaks through,
In sharing pain, our spirits renew.
The blessing found in pure embrace,
Transforms our fears to endless grace.

In every wound, a story told,
A testament of hearts so bold.
With love as guide, we face the storm,
Finding solace in each warm form.

Together we rise, hand in hand,
In vulnerability, we understand.
A sacred link, a bond divine,
In our frailty, His love will shine.

In the Temple of Truth

In quiet halls where echoes dwell,
We seek the tales that wisdom tells.
In sacred space, our spirits meet,
The heart's soft whisper, pure and sweet.

With open minds, we search for light,
In shadows cast by doubt and fright.
For truth unveiled holds boundless grace,
In every corner of this place.

Through years of faith and trials faced,
In the temple of truth, we are embraced.
Each lesson learned, a stepping stone,
Leading us back to love we've known.

A humble heart, a listening ear,
In every moment, love draws near.
With every breath, we choose to seek,
In sacred truth, we're made unique.

As prayers ascend on wings of light,
In the temple, our souls ignite.
In the bonds of truth, we find our way,
To walk in love, come what may.

The Celestial Chorus of Identity

In the depths of silence, a voice does arise,
Echoing softly, beneath the vast skies.
Each note a reminder, of the soul's pure light,
Together we gather, in harmony's flight.

Threads of existence, woven in grace,
Every heart's beat, a sacred embrace.
United we stand, in shadows and sun,
A chorus of purpose, forever as one.

Journeys we traverse, each path unique,
Faith in our being, the strength that we seek.
Through trials and triumphs, our spirits will soar,
In the choir of life, we sing evermore.

The stars are our witnesses, the heavens our guide,
In the dance of existence, we walk side by side.
With love as our anthem, we conquer the strife,
As we find our true selves, in the song of our life.

Trust in the Divine Within

In the stillness of dawn, hear the whisper so clear,
A promise of guidance, always so near.
Trust in the journey, let spirit unfold,
For within every heart, lies a story untold.

Mountains may crumble, and oceans may roar,
Yet the flame of faith, burns stronger than before.
With each step we take, let the light of love lead,
Trust in the divine, for it's all that we need.

In shadows and trials, find strength to arise,
The spark of the divine, ignites in our eyes.
When doubt clouds the mind, remember the truth,
The spirit within, is the fountain of youth.

Surrender to grace, let go of the strife,
For each moment, dear soul, is a gift of this life.
Trust in the heartbeat, the rhythm so sweet,
In the dance of the cosmos, we find our own beat.

My Soul, a Divine Vessel

Within me resides, a vessel of dreams,
Filled with the essence, of light's gentle beams.
Each drop of pure love, a treasure within,
A sacred reminder, where all journeys begin.

Through trials of spirit, I sail on this sea,
With faith as my anchor, forever I'll be.
Embrace of the cosmos, cradled in grace,
In the heart of my vessel, I find my true place.

Let waters of wisdom flow freely through me,
Guiding each ripple, in sync with the sea.
For my soul is a vessel, both humble and grand,
Carrying whispers from the Creator's own hand.

With gratitude soaring, I journey each day,
In the currents of life, I trust and I sway.
My vessel, a beacon, to others in need,
For within every soul, lies the divine seed.

Reflections of Belief

In the mirror of faith, I see all that I am,
A tapestry woven, in the Creator's plan.
Each thread holds a story, a glimpse of the light,
Reflections of belief, shining ever so bright.

What I choose to nurture, grows greater each day,
For thoughts become actions, in a beautiful way.
With every affirmation, I carve my own path,
Reflections of love, in joy and in wrath.

When shadows fall quickly, and doubts start to breed,
I look to the heavens, for strength in my need.
In whispers of grace, my spirit takes flight,
Reflections of belief, a beacon of light.

As stars shine above, illuminating the night,
I align with my essence, and welcome the light.
In the dance of existence, I find my own voice,
Reflections of belief, a sacred choice.

Radiance Revealed

In stillness blooms the light,
A whisper deep within the soul.
With each breath, the truth ignites,
Guiding us towards the whole.

In shadows cast by doubt and fear,
The heart finds courage in its plea.
Trust the path, though not so clear,
For grace will set the spirit free.

Awake, O soul, to dawn's embrace,
Each morning brings a sacred chance.
To see the love in every space,
And join the universe's dance.

Radiance shines from every scar,
A testament of trials faced.
In unity, we find how far,
We've traveled, woven in His grace.

Embrace the light, let shadows go,
With open arms, we claim our share.
In every heart, the radiance flows,
A promise lingers in the air.

The Psalm of My Journey

In valleys low, where sorrows tread,
I walk with faith to guide my way.
Each step a note, a prayer unsaid,
In every moment, grace will stay.

The mountains rise, a daunting sight,
Yet strength within begins to soar.
For in the dark, there shines a light,
A whisper urging me to more.

Through trials vast, my spirit grows,
With every tear, a seed is sown.
In every heartache, wisdom flows,
For life's true path is never lone.

In fellowship, my burdens shared,
With angels walking by my side.
Together, love's warm gaze declared,
As faith's embrace becomes my guide.

So let my song resound and sway,
In harmony with all that's true.
For each day's breath, a chance to pray,
The journey sacred, ever new.

Sacred Steps Towards Clarity

With open heart, I seek the way,
In silence, truth begins to rise.
Each sacred step, a choice to stay,
Awakening the inner skies.

The noise subsides, the spirit hears,
A gentle nudge, the path unfolds.
Through whispered winds, dispelling fears,
The light of wisdom softly holds.

In nature's grace, I find my peace,
Each leaf a scripture in the breeze.
With every breath, my soul's release,
Unveils the wonders of His keys.

Embrace the still, the world will fade,
In presence lies the holy ground.
As blessings flow, no need for trade,
For clarity in love is found.

Let every step, a dance of grace,
In harmony with heaven's song.
The journey's light, a warm embrace,
As sacred hearts will lead us strong.

The Guardian of My Heart

In shadows deep, Your light I seek,
A guiding hand, a steady flame.
When doubts arise, I feel so weak,
With whispered love, You call my name.

O Guardian, my soul's delight,
In every trial, You stand so near.
You turn the dark into the light,
And calm my every hidden fear.

Through storms that rage and winds that howl,
Your presence brings the sweetest peace.
In faith, I trust, I wear the cowl,
Of hope, which gives my heart release.

With every heartbeat, I am known,
In You, my refuge, safe and sound.
In tender love, I have grown,
For in Your arms, my heart is found.

O Guardian, l cherish each glance,
For in Your grace, my spirit's free.
A sacred bond, a holy dance,
In every moment, You and me.

The Crucible of Love and Forgiveness

In the flame where hearts collide,
Grace abounds, our souls abide.
Forgive the wounds that time has scored,
Embrace the light, our spirits soared.

Boundless mercy, endless might,
Transforming pain to purest light.
In love's embrace, we find our way,
A testament of hope each day.

The weight of burdens lifts away,
With every tear, we learn to pray.
In unity, our hearts ignite,
Forgiveness blooms in sacred night.

We wander paths where shadows dwell,
Yet in forgiveness lies the well.
A tree of life, where kindness grows,
In love's embrace, eternity flows.

Through trials faced and battles won,
In love and care, we are but one.
This crucible molds our very souls,
Forgiveness guides, it makes us whole.

In the Sanctuary of Self

In quiet place, the heart can hear,
The gentle whispers drawing near.
In solitude, the spirit sings,
Within our depths, the stillness brings.

With open arms, we seek the light,
In the shadows of the night.
Cultivating peace, we inhale grace,
In stillness found, we find our place.

Reflections dance upon the soul,
In self-discovery, we are whole.
Each breath a prayer, a step in faith,
In the sanctuary, we find our grace.

Through turmoil's storm, we stand our ground,
In inner calm, true strength is found.
Each heartbeat echoes love's decree,
In this haven, we are free.

Nurturing the seeds we've sown,
In self-compassion, we have grown.
Here within, the spirit thrives,
In the sanctuary, love survives.

The Sacred Mirror Within

In each reflection, truth is shown,
A sacred space where love has grown.
We gaze within, our hearts laid bare,
In the mirror's depth, we feel the care.

Fleeting shadows briefly dance,
Yet in the light, we find our chance.
The flaws we see, the beauty too,
In acceptance, our spirits renew.

Through struggles faced, self-love we seek,
In honesty, our hearts grow meek.
Embrace the facets of our grace,
In the mirror's gaze, we find our place.

With every crack, a tale to tell,
In imperfections, we learn to dwell.
The sacred heart, a radiant glow,
In the depths of self, our truth we know.

Explore the depths, the hidden light,
In the sacred mirror, we take flight.
Each journey leads us to begin,
To love ourselves and trust within.

Hymns of Acceptance

In every note, the heart does sing,
A melody of peace we bring.
With open arms, we learn to see,
In acceptance lies our harmony.

Each moment lived, a sacred choice,
In the stillness, we hear the voice.
A symphony of souls aligned,
In unity, our hearts entwined.

Through trials faced, we rise anew,
In understanding, love breaks through.
With every hymn, our spirits soar,
In acceptance, we seek for more.

Embrace the past, yet hold the now,
In gratitude, we solemnly vow.
To cherish life, through joy and pain,
In acceptance, our hearts remain.

We gather round, as one we stand,
In hymns of love, a guiding hand.
Each note a prayer, each word a balm,
In acceptance sweet, we find our calm.

The Rosary of Revelation

In silent prayer, the beads we hold,
Each whispered word, a truth unfolds.
The light that shines, within our soul,
Guides us gently, makes us whole.

As mysteries are shared in grace,
We seek the love that we embrace.
In faith we stand, united strong,
Together, we shall carry on.

Through trials faced, we learn to bend,
The hands of time, our closest friend.
With every tear, a lesson learned,
To hearts ignited, truth is burned.

The rosary reveals our path divine,
A sacred journey, intertwined.
With every prayer, we grow in might,
A beacon bright, in darkest night.

In unity, we find our voice,
A chorus rich, in love we rejoice.
Each bead, a promise, hope we share,
In reverence, we breathe the prayer.

A Testament of Self

In the mirror, I seek to find,
The hidden truths of heart and mind.
With every glance, I dare to see,
The soul within, a mystery.

Through trials faced and battles fought,
In silence, strength is gently caught.
A testament to all I've grown,
In every scar, a seed is sown.

With whispered doubts, the shadows call,
Yet in the dark, I rise, I stand tall.
Embracing flaws, the beauty shines,
For in my heart, divinity aligns.

Each moment lived, a gift bestowed,
In joy and sorrow, love is flowed.
A journey marked by faith and grace,
In every step, I find my place.

From ashes rise, a phoenix flies,
In every truth, the spirit sighs.
A testament, my spirit's song,
In every heart, we all belong.

The Gospel of Inner Strength

In quiet fortitude, I rise,
With every challenge, I reach the skies.
The fire within, a guiding light,
In darkest hours, it burns so bright.

With every breath, I claim my truth,
A testament to love and youth.
In trials faced, my spirit soars,
Each wound endured, my heart restores.

Through storms that rage and winds that howl,
I stand resolute, I do not cowl.
In whispered prayers, I find my might,
The courage within, my endless fight.

As mountains rise, I will ascend,
With faith and hope, I will not bend.
In every struggle, wisdom gained,
A gospel shared, a life unchained.

For in my heart, the strength does dwell,
In life's great dance, I weave my spell.
The gospel sung through joy and strife,
An hymn of love, the song of life.

An Invocation of Identity

With open arms, I call my name,
In echoes deep, I feel the flame.
The essence pure, the spirit free,
An invocation, my truth to be.

In whispers soft, the past unfolds,
A tapestry of stories told.
With every thread, I knit belonging,
A symphony of voices singing.

I stand as one, yet many blend,
In every heartbeat, I comprehend.
The roots I cherish, the wings I own,
In every place, I make my home.

Through trials faced, my identity grows,
In shadows cast, the light still glows.
With every step, I break the mold,
Embracing all, I am, I hold.

An invocation, a sacred vow,
To honor self, to live the now.
In unity of heart and mind,
In every love, my soul I find.

Psalm of the Unfurling Spirit

In the quiet of the dawn, I rise,
With whispers of the wind, I hear,
The light that guides each step I take,
Awakening hope, dispelling fear.

With each breath, I feel the spark,
A flame ignites within my soul,
Connecting me to all that's pure,
In unity, I am made whole.

The mountains echo my sacred song,
The rivers dance with joy divine,
In nature's arms, I find my home,
A tapestry of love entwined.

With fervent heart, I seek the truth,
In shadows dark, the light I find,
Each lesson learned, a step bestowed,
In spirit's grace, I am aligned.

As I unfurl my wings to fly,
In every moment, I am free,
To walk the path that leads me home,
Embracing all that's meant to be.

A Holy Embrace of Identity

In the mirror, I see the light,
Reflecting all that I hold dear,
A canvas bright with colors bold,
Embraced by love, I cast out fear.

Each name I bear, each story shared,
A piece of piecing sacred grace,
In every heartbeat, every breath,
I stand in truth, my rightful place.

With arms wide open to the stars,
I journey forth in gentle peace,
In unity, I find my voice,
A holy chorus, a sweet release.

As seasons change and shadows fade,
I celebrate this life of mine,
In every joy, each tear that falls,
An emblem of the grand design.

So here I stand, a vibrant soul,
Forged from love, divinely made,
In this embrace, I find my truth,
A legacy that will not fade.

Sacred Rituals of Self-Discovery

In silence deep, I turn within,
To seek the light that guides my way,
With every thought, a prayer I weave,
Unraveling doubts, I choose to stay.

Rituals of joy, of breath, of love,
I light a candle, watch it glow,
Each flicker brings me closer still,
To the truest self I yearn to know.

With sacred texts and songs of old,
I gather wisdom from the earth,
In nature's arms, I find the key,
To unlock all my inner worth.

Through journeys wild and paths untamed,
I walk with faith, my spirit bold,
With every step, I claim my truth,
A story rich, a tale retold.

In every challenge, grace appears,
A dance of strength, of love profound,
In this sacred quest, I find my peace,
My spirit soaring, heart unbound.

Threads of Grace in My Essence

Woven softly, threads divine,
In every moment, love's embrace,
The fabric of my life unfolds,
A tapestry of sacred grace.

Each thread a lesson, bright and bold,
A story held within my heart,
In every joy, each tear I shed,
An artful dance, a work of art.

The colors blend, the patterns shift,
In harmony, I find my blend,
With every stitch, my spirit sings,
This journey's path, a sacred bend.

With gratitude, I weave my way,
A heart in tune with life's great flow,
In every breath, I feel the grace,
Interwoven hope, a gentle glow.

So here I stand, a piece bestowed,
In unity with all that's true,
In threads of grace, I find my soul,
A vibrant life, forever new.

The Illuminated Path to Self

In the silence of the night, we seek,
Guided by the flame, so gentle, so meek.
Whispers of truth dance upon the air,
Illuminating shadows of doubt and despair.

With every step, the spirit ignites,
Brightening the journey, revealing the sights.
The heart of the seeker aligns with the stars,
Embracing the wisdom that's hidden in scars.

Each footprint's a story, each breath a prayer,
The path unfurls with love beyond compare.
In unity with nature, we rise and we fall,
On the illuminated path, we answer the call.

Transcending the mirror, we find our place,
Reflections of beauty, the divine we embrace.
In hushed reverence, we walk side by side,
With the light of the soul, our faithful guide.

So let us journey, with hearts open wide,
On this sacred path, where spirit resides.
In the glow of the dawn, our essence awakes,
On the illuminated path, true free will remakes.

Anointed by Acceptance

In the cradle of grace, acceptance blooms,
Whispers of mercy, dispelling the glooms.
Anoint me with kindness, let love overflow,
In the heart's sacred garden, let compassion grow.

With arms wide open, we gather the strays,
Embracing the fallen, in myriad ways.
Our differences woven in God's gentle hand,
Together we flourish, like flowers we stand.

In the warmth of inclusion, all burdens release,
As shadows of judgment dissolve into peace.
Each soul is a mirror, reflecting the light,
Anointed by love, we emerge from the night.

In the symphony of voices, we find our song,
A melody sweet, where all souls belong.
So let us unite in this sacred affair,
Anointed by acceptance, a gift we can share.

With every embrace, divinity shines,
As we honor the journey, in intricate lines.
Anointed, awakened, in purest delight,
In the arms of the cosmos, in love's boundless light.

The Graces of Self-Realization

In the mirror of truth, we face our own grace,
Peeling back layers, time cannot erase.
With courage we rise, as shadows unfold,
The beauty of being, more precious than gold.

Through trials and triumphs, the spirit finds strength,
In the labyrinth of time, we traverse great lengths.
Awakening softly, like dawn's gentle kiss,
In the heart of the storm, we discover our bliss.

In moments of stillness, we listen, we learn,
The graces of self, to the spirit return.
Each heartbeat a promise, each breath a song,
In the arms of realization, we finally belong.

With faith as our compass, and love as our guide,
We walk through the valley, with joy as our stride.
Unraveling fears, we embrace who we are,
In the graces of self, we shine like a star.

So let us ascend, in the light of our truth,
Nourished by wisdom, the essence of youth.
The graces of self-realization arise,
In the tapestry of life, where the spirit never dies.

The Temple of True Being

In the quiet of the soul, a temple stands tall,
Crafted of love, embracing us all.
Within sacred walls, echoes of grace,
Whisper the secrets of our rightful place.

With each gentle heartbeat, the spirit ignites,
Transforming our fears into luminous lights.
The essence of being, a flame ever bright,
Guiding our journey through the shadow of night.

In rituals of kindness, we gather in peace,
Offering prayers for suffering's release.
The temple of being, where all hearts unite,
Sowing seeds of compassion, cultivating light.

Through laughter and tears, we honor the past,
In the temple of true being, connections hold fast.
As branches entwine, in the great cosmic sea,
We discover the miracle of simply being free.

So with each passing day, let us nurture this space,
In the temple of true being, live with grace.
As we breathe in the love, and exhale the fear,
In this sacred sanctuary, our truth is made clear.

Sanctified Shadows

In shadows cast by holy light,
We find our path in darkest night.
With whispered prayers, our souls align,
In sacred trust, His love divine.

The echoes of a soft embrace,
Reach deep, revealing sacred grace.
Each tear that falls, a seed of faith,
In shadows, we shall find our place.

Through trials faced and burdens borne,
In sacred silence, we are reborn.
The shadowed vale shall guide our way,
In stillness, find the light of day.

With every breath, a song of praise,
In every heart, the spirit stays.
Embrace the light, let shadows cease,
In faith, we find our lasting peace.

Together in this journey shared,
With holy love, we shall be spared.
In shadows, hope will cast its glow,
For in His arms, our spirits grow.

Revelations of Resilience

In the silence of our fears,
Awake the strength through trials near.
Each struggle brings a lesson clear,
In resilience, we persevere.

Through storms that test our weary souls,
We rise anew, as faith unfolds.
With every wound, a tale is spun,
In shadows deep, the light is won.

Each tear, a testament of grace,
In every heartbeat, find Your place.
The whispers of Your love sustain,
In humble trust, we break the chain.

When doubt encroaches, hold us tight,
Illuminate the darkest night.
For through the struggle, we shall see,
In revelations, we are free.

Together bound by holy truth,
In trials fierce, unveil our youth.
With courage fierce, we shall arise,
In resilience, reach for the skies.

The Serene Gospel of Self-Acceptance

In silent prayer, we seek the truth,
The gentle echo of our youth.
Embrace the soul, both soft and strong,
In self-acceptance, we belong.

With every flaw, a beauty shines,
In humble grace, the heart defines.
The gospel whispers in the breeze,
Acceptance blooms like gentle trees.

From ashes rise, the spirit learns,
In reflecting light, the heart yearns.
To love ourselves, a holy creed,
In acceptance, find our seed.

Through trials faced and shadows cast,
We find the love that holds us fast.
In gratitude, our spirits soar,
In self-acceptance, we restore.

Together in this sacred space,
We nurture hearts with gentle grace.
The serene gospel flows within,
In love's embrace, we begin again.

The Covenant of the Heart

In quiet vows beneath the skies,
We pledge our love, where spirit flies.
A covenant forged in sacred trust,
In every heartbeat, love is just.

With open arms, the world awaits,
A dance of souls through heaven's gates.
In unity, our hearts shall sing,
The promise of what love can bring.

Through trials faced, through joy and pain,
This covenant shall ever reign.
With every step upon the earth,
Renew our bond, embrace our worth.

In echoes of Your holy name,
Our hearts aflame, we feel no shame.
With every prayer, a vow so true,
In covenant, I stand with You.

Together, hand in hand we walk,
In whispered hopes, our spirits talk.
The covenant of love we share,
In sacred union, we declare.

Meditations in Solitude

In silence, the soul starts to bloom,
Whispers of truth dispel the gloom.
Stars reflect a divine embrace,
In solitude, we find our place.

Stillness cradles the heart's deep sigh,
Each moment unfolds, none can deny.
As shadows dance in flickering light,
We meet the divine, pure and bright.

Embrace the still; let worries cease,
In quietness lies the path to peace.
The breath of the earth sounds a hymn,
In this sacred space, I swim.

In the depth of the night, wisdom glows,
The essence of love tenderly flows.
Each thought a prayer, each tear a song,
In solitude, we learn to belong.

The Sacred Threshold of Be-ing

At the threshold, I bow my head,
Listening keenly to what is said.
Life's tapestry woven with grace,
I feel the divine, in every space.

Each heartbeat a rhythm, a sacred call,
Beyond the silence, we rise or fall.
In the stillness, I find my way,
A journey of trust, come what may.

Hands open wide to the heavens above,
Inviting the flow of everlasting love.
In every moment, I dare to see,
The sacred gift of just being free.

The threshold whispers, do not fear,
The light within is always near.
Step forward gently, embrace the light,
In this sacred dance, all is right.

Epiphanies in Stillness

In the quiet hour, visions blend,
Through the stillness, thoughts ascend.
A flicker of truth in a gentle breath,
Illumination found in the dance of death.

The sacred pause invites the heart,
To revel in art where echoes start.
Each sigh holds wisdom, an ancient song,
In the silence, we know we belong.

Moments of stillness, like jewels, shine,
Transforming the mundane into the divine.
Graces enlightened, like rain on the seed,
In the depths of quiet, the soul is freed.

Here in the hush, the spirit awakes,
A tapestry woven with each step it takes.
Epiphanies bloom in soft twilight,
In stillness, we find our inner light.

Revelations of the Spirit

In the dawn of a new day, hope is reborn,
Promises linger, the spirit is worn.
Each revelation, a gentle guide,
Urging the soul to rise, to glide.

Through trials and shadows, we journey on,
Finding the strength when all seems gone.
In the whispers of night, the truth does shine,
Revelations of spirit, forever divine.

Lost in the chaos, a voice calls clear,
Reminding our hearts to hold what is dear.
Each tear we shed, a story unfolds,
In the light of compassion, the spirit holds.

Awaken to wonders that lie within,
In the depths of a heart, new worlds begin.
Revelations in love, ever profound,
In the spirit's embrace, we are found.

Gospel of Resilience and Faith

In shadows deep, our hearts still rise,
A beacon shines, through night it cries.
With every fall, we learn to stand,
For grace envelops, a guiding hand.

The trials come, like storms so fierce,
Yet from the pain, our spirits pierce.
A garden grows in barren soil,
With hope reborn, we find our toil.

In whispers soft, the truth does dwell,
Each prayer a bell, that breaks the shell.
Our voices rise like thunder's roar,
In unity we find the core.

The journey long, with faith as guide,
In darkest night, He stands beside.
With resilience bright, we face our fate,
A heart of love will never wait.

So let us lift, our eyes to grace,
In every wound, we find His face.
The gospel sings, through every breath,
In life, in love, we conquer death.

The Light Within the Wilderness

Amidst the trees where silence breathes,
A light ignites, a flame that weaves.
Through tangled paths and skies so grey,
The heart will find its way to stay.

In barren lands, the spirit seeks,
A voice of hope, when courage peaks.
With every step, a promise glows,
Like rivers flow, our faith bestows.

The wilderness, a sacred ground,
Where whispers soft, in stillness found.
In shadows long, the light does play,
Revealing truths, night turns to day.

O traveler lost, embrace the night,
For in the dark, He brings the light.
Within the trials, the soul will rise,
With faith as wings, it learns to fly.

As stars above etch paths divine,
We walk with grace, our hearts align.
In every breath, the wilderness sings,
For in His love, we find our wings.

Manuscript of the Soul's Journey

In every heart, a story dwells,
A manuscript where truth compels.
With ink of life, each moment penned,
The soul's voyage has no end.

Through valleys low, and hills of grace,
We find ourselves in time and space.
Each tear a word, each smile a line,
In sacred rhythms, stars align.

The parchment worn, yet brightly shines,
With wisdom gained in sacred signs.
Each trial faced, like pages turned,
In every loss, new lessons learned.

The chapters flow, like rivers wide,
In faith we write, through joy and pride.
The ink may fade, yet still we cling,
To every song, our spirits sing.

So let us pen, with hope imbued,
The manuscript of love renewed.
For in this tale, the light is cast,
A journey bold, forever lasts.

Sacred Echoes of Self-Truth

In silence deep, the echoes call,
A whisper soft, within us all.
Each sacred heart, a story true,
In layers deep, we find the view.

With every breath, the truth unfolds,
A tapestry of dreams and golds.
The voice of pain, the song of grace,
In every trial, we find our place.

With courage strong, we rise anew,
To face the world, a brighter hue.
In self-reflection, wisdom grows,
The garden blooms, where love overflows.

So let us tread, with hearts ablaze,
In sacred truths, we set the gaze.
For in the echoes, we create
A legacy of love, our fate.

As light descends, and shadows sway,
We honor truth, in night and day.
In every echo, let us find,
The sacred song that binds mankind.

Manifesting the Divine Within

In silence, whispers softly dwell,
The light within, a sacred well.
With every breath, a prayer is sung,
Awakening truth, old yet young.

In shadows cast, the spirit grows,
Through trials faced, the heart bestows.
A spark ignites, the soul in trance,
With courage bright, we take our chance.

The canvas laid, our faith we draw,
In love's embrace, we find the law.
Every heartbeat echoes grace,
As we reveal our holy space.

With hands outstretched, we seek the way,
In gratitude, the dawn of day.
The divine within, a cherished guide,
In humble bow, our hearts confide.

Together we rise, the veil now torn,
In unity, the spirit's born.
From depths of soul, we manifest,
The divine light, our truest quest.

The Quietude of Divine Acceptance

In stillness found, a gentle grace,
The heart unfolds, a sacred space.
With each exhale, the worries fade,
In presence deep, our fears are laid.

The whispers of the soul arise,
In quietude, the spirit flies.
With open arms, we greet the night,
In trust divine, we find the light.

In every tear, a lesson learned,
In every joy, our spirits burned.
Acceptance blooms, the heart's delight,
In unity, we hold the fight.

The path ahead, uncertain yet clear,
With faith as anchor, we persevere.
In silence pure, the mind lets go,
In divine love, our spirits grow.

Together in this tranquil realm,
We rise as one, each at the helm.
With hearts entwined, we softly tread,
In quietude, our souls are fed.

A Testament of Inner Wholeness

In shadows danced, the light reveals,
A testament of what life feels.
With every scar and every grace,
We weave the threads of the human race.

A harmony sings, within the soul,
Each piece embraced, we become whole.
Through trials faced, we learn to be,
In perfect flaws, we set us free.

The universe within each heart,
In love's embrace, we find our part.
Through kindness shown, the spirit soars,
In giving self, the heart restores.

The journey bright, each step we take,
A map of love, the road we make.
In sacred trust, our truths align,
With every breath, the stars will shine.

In unity, we rise as one,
A testament, the work begun.
Through inner peace, we understand,
Together strong, we make our stand.

The Ascension of Self-Awareness

In moments still, we turn within,
A journey starts, the quest begins.
With every thought, a seed is sown,
In awareness gained, the truth is known.

From silent depths, the spirit calls,
In self-reflection, the shadow falls.
Each layer peeled, the heart's embrace,
Revealing light in every space.

Amidst the noise, a sacred hum,
In quietude, our essence comes.
With open eyes, the world transforms,
In self-awareness, new life forms.

In every heartbeat, wisdom flows,
The path ahead, the spirit shows.
With courage bold, we seek to see,
The beauty found in simply being.

Together we rise, as one we grow,
The light of self, a vibrant glow.
In every heart, the truth ignites,
The ascension of our inner sights.

The Divine Tapestry of Being

In threads of grace, we weave our fate,
Each moment precious, love innate.
The fabric bright with colors vast,
A sacred bond, forever cast.

Through trials faced, we seek the light,
In darkness deep, we find our sight.
The hands of time, both kind and bold,
Unravel stories yet untold.

Beneath the stars, our spirits sing,
A chorus sweet, to life we cling.
In every heart, a spark divine,
The essence pure, forever shine.

Together bound by fate's embrace,
We journey on, the human race.
With faith adorned, we walk our path,
In love's embrace, we find our half.

Each soul a note in harmony,
A symphony of unity.
In the silence, whispers clear,
The truth of being, ever near.

Illuminated by Inner Light

In the stillness of the night,
A spark ignites, our inner light.
With every breath, a gentle glow,
A guiding star, we come to know.

Through shadows cast, we seek the flame,
In hearts ablaze, we find our name.
The truth of self, so pure and bright,
A radiant path, our souls take flight.

In silence deep, the spirit stirs,
A whisper soft, love's voice occurs.
Through trials faced, we stand in grace,
Embracing all, in this sacred space.

With every heart that opens wide,
Together we walk, side by side.
In unity, our spirits rise,
To greet the dawn, with joyful sighs.

Illuminated by love's embrace,
In every soul, we see His face.
Forever kind, the light we share,
A living testament to care.

Sanctuary of the Heart's Truth

In the sanctuary where love abides,
A sacred space, where grace resides.
Each heartbeat echoes, pure and clear,
A refuge found, forever near.

Here, in silence, the spirit speaks,
With gentle whispers, peace it seeks.
In every tear, in every smile,
The truth unfolds, transcending miles.

Through trials faced, our hearts will mend,
In this embrace, we find a friend.
The power lies in what we feel,
A bond so deep, it starts to heal.

Together we rise, on wings of trust,
In love unbound, we find the must.
The heart's truth sings, in harmony,
Our souls unite, forever free.

In this sanctuary, joy will bloom,
Dispelling darkness, chasing gloom.
With open hearts, we come to be,
In love's embrace, eternally.

The Gospel of Self-Love

In the gospel of love, we learn to see,
The beauty within, the truth of we.
With open arms, we greet the day,
In kindness spoken, we find our way.

Through trials faced, we rise anew,
In every act, self-love shines through.
With every breath, we claim our worth,
A sacred truth, our place on Earth.

In whispers soft, the heart takes flight,
As shadows fade, we embrace the light.
Each moment cherished, a gift to hold,
In self-acceptance, our story's told.

Together we walk, hand in hand,
In love's embrace, we understand.
A journey long, yet sweetly shared,
In every heart, we know we're cared.

The gospel sings in every voice,
In self-love found, we make the choice.
To rise together, hearts ablaze,
In love's reflection, we sing His praise.

The Seraphim Within

In shadows deep, the light does sing,
Seraphim whisper, on angel's wing.
Graceful bold, they lift my soul,
Guiding me toward the sacred whole.

In quiet prayer, their voices rise,
Awakening hope beneath dark skies.
Each feathered note, a divine embrace,
Awakens love, illumines grace.

Within my heart, their fire glows,
Fueling faith, where wisdom flows.
Dancing stars in celestial flight,
Reveal the path, show me the light.

In turmoil, they bring gentle peace,
With sacred words, my fears release.
A holy chorus, their anthem true,
Reminding me of what's pure and due.

The seraphim dwell, no distance far,
They shine through me, my guiding star.
In every breath, I sense their grace,
With joy I dwell in this holy place.

Revelations from the Depths

In the silence, truths emerge,
From the depths, my soul I purge.
Waves of wisdom gently rise,
Unveiling secrets, ancient ties.

Beneath the surface, shadows creep,
Yet in the darkness, light will seep.
Voices of ages echo clear,
In whispers soft, I draw them near.

Revelations dance like flames at night,
Illuminating doubts with light.
The journey's long, but I will find,
The sacred truth, the divine kind.

With every heartbeat, lessons bloom,
Breaking free from chains of gloom.
In surrender, my spirit wakes,
In every breath, the promise shakes.

In depths unknown, my heart will fly,
With open wings, I seek the sky.
Each revelation, a sacred boon,
Guiding me closer to the moon.

Communion with My Inner Light

In stillness found, the spirit speaks,
Whispers soft, the heart it seeks.
The sacred spark, a flame divine,
Illuminating paths that intertwine.

Within the quiet, wisdom stirs,
Embracing me, as silence purrs.
In every breath, I feel the glow,
A tender warmth, my faith will grow.

Communion deep, my inner sight,
Reveals the world in radiant light.
In moments rare, I pause and see,
The endless love alive in me.

With humble heart, I open wide,
To join the dance, the faithful tide.
In unity, our spirits soar,
Together strong, forevermore.

As dawn unfolds, I rise anew,
Bathed in light, and all I do.
A shining truth, a hallowed song,
Within my heart, where I belong.

The Offering of My True Nature

In quiet moments, I discern,
The essence pure, for which I yearn.
A humble heart, an open hand,
I offer all, I make my stand.

The depths of soul, I freely share,
In every thought, I seek to care.
With gratitude, I lift my gaze,
Embracing life in endless praise.

The offering flows, like rivers wide,
In kindness rich, I take the stride.
Each moment passed, a sacred gift,
In giving, I embrace the lift.

With every breath, I sow the seed,
Of love and hope, in thought and deed.
In every act, my spirit flies,
Awakening grace, beneath the skies.

The true nature behind the veil,
In vulnerability, I shall not fail.
Together we rise, with hearts ablaze,
In sharing love, we find our ways.

Milton Keynes UK
Ingram Content Group UK Ltd.
UKHW031321271124
451618UK00007B/159